TRADITIONAL CHINESE TEXTILE DESIGNS
IN FULL COLOR

Edited by the
Research Studio of the
Northeast Drama Institute
People's Republic of China

Dover Publications, Inc.
New York

PUBLISHER'S NOTE

Traditional Chinese opera, though aspects of it vary from region to region, is always a highly stylized drama incorporating rhythmic instrumental accompaniment and vocal recitative and song, and often featuring dance and acrobatics. The subjects are usually drawn from history, legend or classic novels.

Just as the movements and gestures of the actors follow age-old patterns, so their physical appearance is strictly controlled. Although Chinese opera uses relatively few props and practically no scenery, the performer's makeup and costume are elaborate. Wigs and face painting reveal the personality traits of the character being portrayed; the costume proclaims his rank in society or indicates his permanent or temporary occupation. (Certain elements of the costume, especially the sleeves, also aid the actor in expressing states of mind and emotions.)

The costumes are richly embroidered with traditional motifs in colored silk and cotton and gold and silver thread. The immediately recognizable motifs, which occupy specifically prescribed positions on the various types of garments, frequently serve as symbols or emblems. For instance, such noble creatures as dragons and lions are suitable for emperors, ministers and high officials. The phoenix, which represents peace and good fortune, but also feminine beauty, is often found on women's robes. Pairs of mandarin ducks, emblems of conjugal bliss, appear on bride's clothing. Cranes symbolize longevity; the lotus, purity amid a sinful world; the peony, wealth and honor; plum blossoms, the return of spring. The bat, through a play on words, stands for happiness.

The present volume reproduces sixty of these beautiful and meaningful motifs, as rendered in authentic color by the artists Lu Hua and Ma Chiang for an official publication in Peking. It is interesting to note the varying degrees of abstraction encountered in different versions of one and the same motif. Also instructive is the ingenuity with which the motifs have been adapted to their specific use on the garment: as circular "crests" for broad, flat areas, and as elongated panels for borders, collars and trouser legs. The captions identify each motif and briefly indicate the type of costume, and the parts of that costume, on which they occur.

FRONT COVER: Dragon. For the front and back of a dragon robe (*mang*). BACK COVER: Phoenixes. For the collar and sleeve borders of a woman's informal robe (*pei*).

Copyright © 1980 by Dover Publications, Inc.
All rights reserved under Pan American and International Copyright Conventions.

Published in Canada by General Publishing Company, Ltd., 30 Lesmill Road, Don Mills, Toronto, Ontario.
Published in the United Kingdom by Constable and Company, Ltd., 10 Orange Street, London WC2H 7EG.

Traditional Chinese Textile Designs in Full Color is a new selection of plates from the portfolio *Designs on Chinese Opera Costumes / Edited by the Research Studio of the Northeast Drama Institute / Designs Reproduced by Lu Hua and Ma Chiang*, as published by the People's Art Publishing House, Peking, in 1957. The Publisher's Note and captions have been prepared specially for the Dover edition, incorporating data from the English-language booklet issued with the portfolio.

The first Dover edition of this work was published under the title *Full-Color Designs from Chinese Opera Costumes*.

DOVER *Pictorial Archive* SERIES

International Standard Book Number: 0-486-23979-9
Library of Congress Catalog Card Number: 79-54000

Manufactured in the United States of America
Dover Publications, Inc.
180 Varick Street
New York, N.Y. 10014

Phoenix. For the front and back of a woman's ordinary robe (*hsueh tse*).

The character for longevity. For the front, back and sleeves of a woman's informal robe (*pei*).

The character for longevity encircled by five bats; the total composition stands for "five blessings and long life." For the front, back and sleeves of an informal robe (*pei*).

Chrysanthemum. For the skirt of a woman's ordinary robe (*hsueh tse*).

Chrysanthemums. For the front, back and sleeves of a woman's ordinary robe (*hsueh tse*).

Two phoenixes. For the front, back and sleeves of a woman's informal robe (*pei*).

Two dragons playing with a pearl. For the front, back and sleeves of an informal robe (*pei*).

LEFT: Lotus. RIGHT: Chrysanthemum. Both for the sleeves of an ordinary robe (*hsueh tse*).

Two renditions of peonies. For the collar of an ordinary robe (*hsueh tse*).

Lion playing with a ball. For the front, back and sleeves of an official's informal robe (*kai chang*).

Dragon. For the front of a dragon robe (*mang*).

Pear blossoms. For the collar, sleeve borders and skirt border of an ancient dress.

Chrysanthemums. For the collar and hem of a woman's jacket and trouser legs.

Phoenix. For the front, back and sleeves of a woman's informal robe (*pei*).

Phoenix. For the front, back and sleeves of a woman's informal robe (*pei*).

LEFT: Chrysanthemum. RIGHT: Camellia. Both for the sleeves of an ordinary robe (*hsueh tse*).

LEFT: Peony. RIGHT: Leaves and fruit of the nandin (sacred bamboo). Both for the sleeves of an
ordinary robe (*hsueh tse*).

17

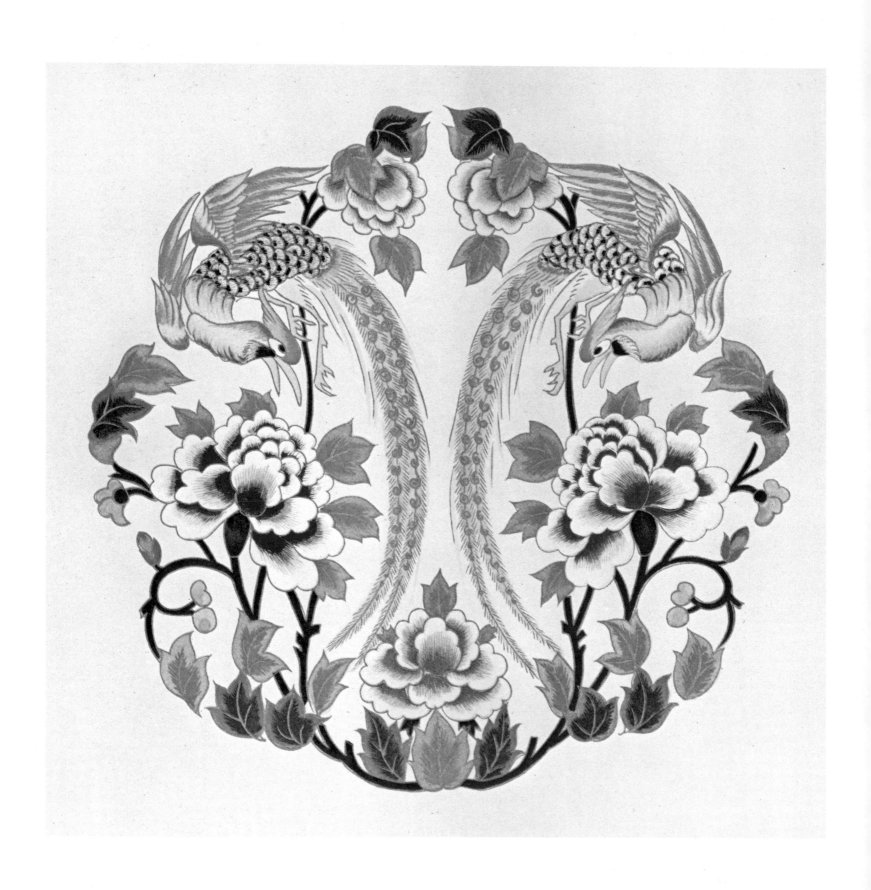

Phoenixes and peonies. For the front, back and sleeves of a woman's informal robe (*pei*).

Mandarin ducks and lotus. For the front, back and sleeves of a woman's informal robe (*pei*).

Lion playing with a ball. For the front, back and sleeves of an official's informal robe (*kai chang*).

Dragon. For the front, back and sleeves of an official's informal robe (*kai chang*).

Phoenix. For the front and back of a woman's informal robe (*pei*).

Phoenix. For the front and back of a woman's ordinary robe (*hsueh tse*).

Phoenix on a flowering plum bough. For the front and back of a woman's ordinary robe
(*hsueh tse*).

Butterflies. For the front and back of a woman's jacket.

LEFT: Monthly rose. RIGHT: Wisteria. Both for the border of a woman's ordinary robe (*hsueh tse*).

cessful illustrations, the magazine signed the artist up for fifty detailed covers a year, including the creation of the image of Doc Savage, one of the adventure magazines' most memorable and enduring heroes. Baumhofer explained that the editors of the magazine wanted Savage to resemble Clark Gable, but Baumhofer chose instead a more personal vision of the hero. It was also at this time that Baumhofer began to experiment with a looser, more painterly style in his work for Popular Publications. Following this period, Baumhofer became associated with *Liberty Magazine* and what the artist calls "the classier slicks" for whom he has worked as a

Walter M. Baumhofer
upper left: *THE LYNCHING, oil/canvas, 23 x 23, Created for* **American Weekly**
left: *BASEBALL OPENING DAY, oil/board, 25 x 21, Created for* **American Weekly***, Collection C. Woodsby*
above: *THE STAMPEDE, casein/canvas, 18½ x 24½, Created for* **Argosy**

master illustrator over the past 35 years.

While Baumhofer's career marks him as a prolific and successful master illustrator of the great age of American adventure magazines, he also deserves and has found a place with the very few illustrators who see and approach their work as being in the mainstream of serious American painting. Walter Baumhofer represents today the unique American illustrator as artist.

Baumhofer's abilities are best seen in his highly skilled line and masterly use of color. Even small sketches used as preliminary designs contain a power and strength that separates Baumhofer from the artist who merely describes action. Like the great painters who preceded him, Baumhofer's art is firmly rooted in the serious traditions of American painting. His ability to create a mood lifts his work into a special category of painting designed to create, and not merely record, the energy or action of a moment.

Walter Baumhofer is a past member of the Society of Illustrators, where

he had a one-man exhibition in 1941. He has also been included in a number of group exhibitions there. His work has been widely exhibited at galleries and art spaces throughout the United States, including the Brooklyn Museum in 1942. A major retrospective of his work is scheduled for a tour in the State of Florida in 1982 and will open at the Museum of Arts and Sciences in Daytona Beach, Florida, the sponsors of the tour. Baumhofer's work is contained in a host of public and private collections including the Custer Museum in Monroe, Michigan; The Riveredge Foundation, Calgary, Canada; and the Cashi Collection located in Orlando, Florida.

The artist is currently well represented in major resource material on American artists and illustrators including *Who's Who in American Art, Artists of the American West,* the *Cambridge International Biography* and *The Illustrator in America,* and will no doubt earn a lasting place in the future histories of this important period of American art and expression. ∎

Two renditions of chrysanthemums. Both for the collar of an ordinary robe (*hsueh tse*).

Peony. For the front, back and sleeves of a woman's informal robe (*pei*).

Peony. For the front, back and sleeves of an informal robe (*pei*).

Flower, fish and bat. For the hanging border of a warrior's tunic (*pao yi*).

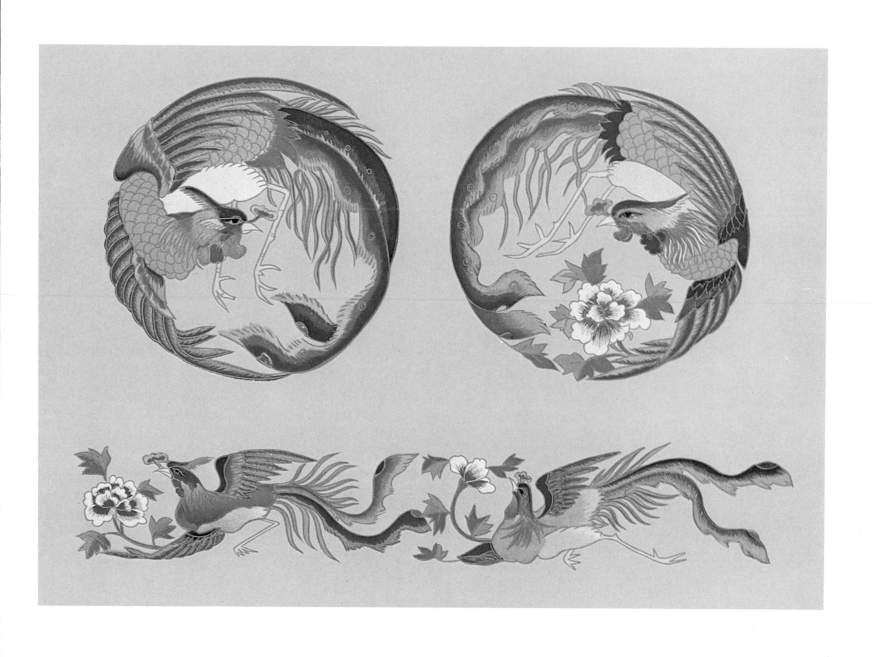

Phoenixes. For the front, back and sleeves of a woman's informal robe (*pei*).

Phoenix and flowers. For the front and back of a woman's informal robe (*pei*).

Kingfishers and peony. For the front and back of a woman's informal robe (*pei*).

Lotus. For the skirt of an ordinary robe (*hsueh tse*).

LEFT: Apricot blossoms. CENTER: Day lilies. RIGHT: Pear blossoms. All for the legs of a
woman's trousers.

Crane. For the front, back and sleeves of an official's crane robe (*ho chang*).

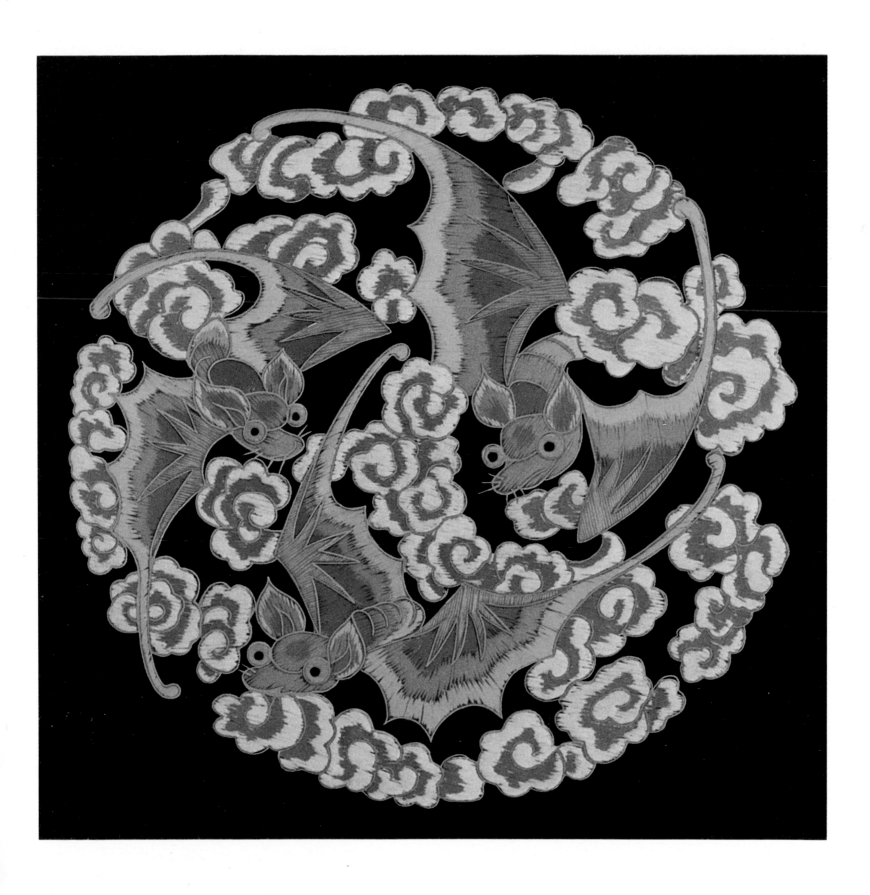

Bats among clouds, representing "blessings from heaven." For the front and back of a
traveling garment (*chien yi*).

Two lions playing with a ball. For the front and back of an ordinary robe (*hsueh tse*).

Dragon. For the front of a dragon robe (*mang*).

Mandarin ducks and lotus. For the front, back and sleeves of a woman's informal robe (*pei*).

Chrysanthemum. For the front and back of an ordinary robe (*hsueh tse*).

Peony and plum blossoms. For the front, back, sleeves and hem of a woman's informal robe (*pei*).

Cranes. For the front, back and sleeve borders of a woman's informal robe (*pei*).

LEFT: Chrysanthemum. For a skirt border. RIGHT: Peony. For the collar of an ordinary robe
(*hsueh tse*).

LEFT: Chrysanthemum. For the sleeves of a woman's ordinary robe (*hsueh tse*). RIGHT: Peony.
For the collar of a woman's jacket.

Phoenix. For the front, back and sleeves of a woman's informal robe (*pei*).